CHAIR YOGA

A Guided Path
from Fear to Faith

ALBA NAGURNEY

Balboa Press books may be ordered through booksellers or by contacting:

Balboa Press
A Division of Hay House
1663 Liberty Drive
Bloomington, IN 47403
www.balboapress.com
844-682-1282

ISBN: 979-8-7652-4801-0 (sc)
ISBN: 979-8-7652-4800-3 (e)

Library of Congress Control Number: 2023923439

Print information available on the last page.

Balboa Press rev. date: 03/05/2024

BALBOA.PRESS
A DIVISION OF HAY HOUSE

Dedication:
For my parents, who art in heaven.

CONTENTS

CHAPTER 1

Obstacles are Detours in the Right Direction

*"If you knew who walks besides you on the path that
you have chosen, fear would be impossible"*

A Course of Miracles

Are you seeking greater purpose and fulfillment in your life, but find yourself struggling with fear and self-doubt? Maybe a voice inside you that you are unworthy of good things?

You are not alone. I was that person.

Sixteen years ago I had a car accident that changed my life completely.

Until this moment its so clear in my mind, like as if it was yesterday.

I was driving from Laurel, Maryland to Baltimore to the Fallon Federal Office building at Hopkins Plaza to get my green card. It was a sunny day, blue sky and I was so excited to get my green card, and step towards being a citizen of the United States.

As I was driving toward my destiny, I approached an exit with a small curve and a big truck was behind me. Instead of slowing down, he accelerated and when he saw me he used his brakes. But at that point it was too late for him to stop. He hit me from the back and threw my vehicle sideways. This person driving the truck stayed and called an ambulance for me. Paramedics came to assist me coming out of the car. So I was transported in the ambulance to the nearest hospital . I did not have any bleeding. Just felt confused, dizzy and pain in my neck and lower back. So after arriving to the hospital in the ER, they took x-rays of my head and neck to see if I had a fracture in my skull or any vertebrae of the neck.

After a couple of hours of observation; they told me that all the exams were negative, so I could go home and rest. If I developed any symptoms, like headache or vomiting, I needed to come back to the hospital. They gave me muscle relaxants and pain medication and told me to follow up with my doctor.

I did the follow up with my doctor and she told me to start physical therapy as soon as possible which I did. After two months of attending therapy I still had pain; and something new happened to me. I started suffering migraines, which I never had in my life. Maybe an occasional headache, but not migraines. They showed up for me 3 times that week. I went back to my doctor and she gave me a prescribed medication named Sumatriptan 100mgr. I was only to take it when I got the pain, because it can cause addiction.

I started having a rebound pain the next day I had migraines, and at the same time I was feeling very weak. Basically I was suffering with this the whole week.

At that time I was in the retail business of Skin care and Make Up. I was determined to be a business owner and empower women, which I have always been so passionate about.

Yes I did assist women to leave a job that they did not want and generate their own income from home and enjoy more time with their families. The majority of them were single mothers having three jobs, so I was determined to help them in their finances so that they could work from home.

And it happened life was good for everybody. I was traveling to different places due to the different events that this company was holding. Some of the other perks that I got from the company was a car, and other things.

Three months after my accident I could not schedule as many appointments as I could before. When the pain would start I took a Sumatriptan pill and I needed to wait for the effect of dizziness to disappear so that I could drive. It was convenient for me. But not for the schedule of my customers, so I started losing sales and customers.

Every time I had those migraine attacks I needed to be in a dark room, isolated with no noise, because with any external stimulant I felt the pain harder.

My doctor sent me to a neurologist who had assisted a lot of patients with migraine. He gave me a medication that only made me wait more, but didn't decrease the migraines. So I quit that specialist and came back to my regular doctor. He told me to call John Hopkins and ask for an appointment with a specialist. Hopkins has a center just only for migraine patients. So I did call them and they gave me my appointment in two years. I was like "wow," so it means a lot of people are suffering the same like me, and I am not alone in this pain. Well, in fact I was not alone I had Rover with me; a black German shepherd rescued at Upper Marlboro shelter. Every time I was starting to have pain, he sensed it and stayed with me.

I lived with pain for 5 years, I went to chiropractor, acupuncture, I ate a clean diet, turmeric, magnesium. Nothing worked for me.

My doctor sent me for evaluation with the neurosurgeon for evaluation. This doctor told me that I needed to do traction exercises 3 times a day. So basically I needed to buy a device attached to my door, do the exercises. and he would see me in 3 months.

I did what he told me. I found certain relief while I was doing the exercises, but it came back afterwards. So he mentioned to me morphine if the pain continued or to consider surgery.

Everyday I saw my neighbors through my window going to work, having a life, and me just on my couch in pain with Rover.

One afternoon I prayed to God asking for a second opportunity in life, to be healthy and enjoy life.

I told Him I surrender, as I knelt down.

The next morning I woke up and was inspired to go to the internet. I was looking for more healthy recipes as I like to cook. Suddenly I saw an advertisement about yoga and about how so many people were free of pain just to this ancient practice.

So I looked for a yoga studio close to home. I went there and enrolled in yoga classes. Strength and flexibility did not come easy for me. So many poses felt completely impossible. I practiced everyday. I knew that if someone else could do it, so could I, so I never gave up. I did it everyday for 6 months. At that point the pain disappeared; I visited the neurosurgeon and he told me that I did not need surgery anymore. At that moment I felt free, no more doctors, no more medicine. Yoga transformed my life. So I decided to become a yoga instructor to heal the world with yoga. I could collaborate with other healers in the world to do it together, helping people to be free of pain. I began pursuing becoming a yoga instructor and I saw movement that I have never seen before. At that moment something in me was awakened. I was inspired and full of passion.

This is why I practice and this is why I teach.

Knowing you can achieve anything you set your mind to – it's the most empowering feeling. You have the potential to change your body, your mind, even your life. You have the potential to be anything you want be. The impossible is always within reach.

YOGA OF CONSCIOUSNESS (The love in me, salutes the love in you)

According to the Beatles: "All you need is love "

CHAIR YOGA: Love in action: A vehicle for healing and social change. Nonviolent communication.

Love without action is irrelevant; and action without love is meaningless. I invite you to take action.

I have created a dynamic signature program based on the acronym of CHAIR Yoga. This is an inclusive program, it doesn't matter your age, gender, religion. It supports my mission on earth which is to be a channel of love and a conduit for Spiritual Awakening in others and a conduit to generate miracles. My program is a collaborative model. Not competitive, this is the way I found to collaborate with others to co-create. We all have the same purpose; my purpose is your purpose, to love and to be loved. And as The Course of Miracles said: "An idea grows stronger when its shared".

The fruit of love is service, which can be described as compassion in action.

C: Namaste Consciousness, H: Healing A: Breath Awareness, I: Inspired intention, R: Response management

NAMASTE CONSCIOUSNESS:
Living with greater meaning and purpose by increasing our consciousness to the presence of God or a spiritual connection of your own understanding. Consciousness is the level of cause of all things that happen in the world. The Law of Cause and effect is the basic building block of Consciousness and the world we experience. Its a reflection of consciousness. Trying to change the world only on the level of effect is like trying to change the screen in the movie, but you can't do that because these images are projected to the screen. You interpret your life through a script

and a character. Your reactions and patterns show in every moment of your life. You did not take conscious decisions, who acted was your character in automatic mode. Until you recognize this situation and choose consciously, the universe will be sending you the same situation.

Everything we do is infused with the consciousness that we do it. No problem can be solved with the same consciousness that you create it. There are two states of Consciousness: Love and Fear.

The truth of who you are it's love. We are an idea in the mind of God. God is in your mind. Being of the mind of God you have all the attributes of the mind of God. We share the same mind. We are one with God and all humanity. The mind that separates from God is called the ego. It is the split mind, based on the idea that we are separate and that we have to figure out everything. Its the consciousness that dominates the world ; Its a malignant consciousness ; like a cancer cell that is separate from normal cells in the body. You are unclear of who you are, forgetting your connection with God and our connection to each other. This Ego consciousness its related with your inner child; a big percentage of programs that you received consciously or unconsciously in the past.

You have only one decision to make: From where Am I going to act: From love or Fear?

First you need to take consciousness about how you are feeling, being present in your body.

If you do not want how you are feeling you need to change your perception or the way you are proceeding with that situation.

2) Change in the thinking: You give it to the Holy Spirit or your internal teacher. Change the script and the persona and you will have a different result.

3) Ask for help: its a state of surrendering

4) Go beyond your programs and anterior roles, and free yourself

Would you really want to be free?

Would you really want to be the person that you really are:

Make a pause to connect with your internal teacher and silence the Ego; How: By breathing three times, you stop your mind and you give permission to enter the voice of your internal teacher.2), take a glass of water, and then practice these movements an affirmations as I am going to share with you in Chapter 7.

You are so powerful because you are a child of God. The Empowerer of your life comes from knowing

who you are and what are you here for? There is an undeletable file of love in your consciousness, God created, it can not be deleted.

All thoughts create form at some level; every thought that is a thought of love, its a thought of truth to who you are. When you are not thinking with love; it means you are not thinking, at all. Its an illusion. Illusions manifest and are as powerful as the truth. Loneliness thoughts produce fear.

To purify your consciousness to get rid of the clutter and stress through prayer and meditation; spend five minutes with God in the morning; its enough to guarantee you that spirit will be in charge of your thought form during the day. You ground yourself, you do not only purify your body, you purify your consciousness. When you wake up in the morning, make yourself available of what to do, where to go, what to say and to whom to speak; surrendering to God, not to someone outside yourself. The Course of Miracles said "One day you will realize there is nothing outside yourself ". When you ask in any situation May God's will be done. God is love, and God wills its thought (building an attitudinal muscle, through prayer, meditation or do a dedication). "May who I am today be a blessing, May I be a space where other people feel greater possibilities within themselves. The Love in me salutes the love in you." This is The Namaste Consciousness. Setting your subconscious First. Don't go directly in the morning to read your emails, social media or watch the news. If you go into that first, your mind will be imprinted with that, the false belief that we are separate rather than one, and it will seek to destroy you. The problem is addressed by the level of consciousness(cause)you have.

The Holy Spirit dwells in our consciousness, as our internal teacher. A bridge of internal communication between our limiting mind and the unlimited mind of God. Authorized by God to help you to change your mind, as you request the Spirit. Its like a GPS. You tell him; "I got lost, but I need to come back." The answer will come in different ways; for example, it could be a book, a conversation, a thought you had, a friend. But if you do not ask for it; you will not notice it. The Holy Spirit will vibrate through your intelligence. Because when you make yourself fully available to God you will receive instructions more quickly and clearly.

If you have a new project, an idea; avoid the consciousness trying to figure it out. Instead say, "Dear God use me."

The universe is programmed for your highest good and your highest function.

HEALING:

Lets remember the power that we have from love. Healing comes by pointing inward and in the presence of atoning for your own mistakes and forgiving other people for their mistakes. Go into the level of cause where you got it wrong. And the situation will miraculously transform. Shift in the level of perception. From fear to love.

Healing is reconnecting the mind to the intelligence of your body; and being able to repattern your energy. There is intelligence in your body; it's how you were born in this world, When you were a child you felt everything. Then as you move through the world and move through different experiences, you develop defense responses and adaptive patterns. You start to loose access to feeling those parts of yourself.

It takes more energy from your system to push things down and to suppress emotions. Feeling and sensing is your natural state.

My personal healing journey started when I started serving other people teaching Yoga; because when you serving others; it utilizes all of your own stuff.

INSPIRED INTENTION SETTING: It is about how you want to show up in every moment of your life. Intention guides your actions and decisions toward achieving goals, aligning our actions with your values and beliefs. Manifesting your visions into a reality. What energy do you want to bring so that you fulfill a bigger vision of yourself? What do you want to be?

Say one word - what do you want to receive from this book? What are you needing right now? Express it with a word. Maybe write it down. Tune into that word whether its peace, love, connection, abundance, whatever the thing you want to receive. Feel it as it is already a part of you, and I guarantee it. Its already who you are, whatever the word is, its already who you are. A lot of times there is something in the way. So during the breath work session you have an opportunity to see what's in the way, Use the breath to clear it out. Its just like the Rumi quote: "Your task is not to seek to find love or clarity or abundance, your task is any of it. Your task is to clear all the barriers that are in the way."

To remember yourself, during these breath work session you have the opportunity to reconnect with yourself and to clear everything that is in the way. And lot of the time you will find out its who you are.

The intention of the Miracle worker is to do God's will. Reclaiming the truth of who you are, your identity. Its that you are love. Before you go to any situation set your intention from the Consciousness of love. Then through universal laws that intention is matched and opportunities open, possibilities happen. You will see life differently. You are able not only to catch vision but also able to catch wisdom from your soul. and not from external authorities. From each being there is a destiny trying to emerge.

Bless everybody before you are going into a room with love, you take the love from your heart to leave to the hearts of others. When you bless others, you bless yourself.

BREATHE AWARENESS

Breath is one of the most powerful awareness and healing tools you can use to shift out old patterns and rise into who you truly are and what you are capable of living.

Find a comfortable seat and connect with your breathe. Then build a breathe awareness by observing the rise and the fall in your belly. Be aware of what you are feeling with your breathe.

Then take a moment to pause and bring either the right or left hand to your heart. Use whatever hand is comfortable for you. Notice how you feel. Feeling is the language of the body Are you feeling angry, sad, fear or anxiety? Any emotion you must be aware of. If you don't look at it, it will not transcend; The Course of Miracles said: "Look at the crucifixion, but not dwell on it"

Being present and mindful as we interact with others is the first step to engaging in effective communication. We are communal beings, we need each other.

If something overwhelming happened to you in the past, then you disconnect with your true self. Another scenario would be if you were not allowed to be your true self. And if you can not connect with yourself also you can not connect with other people. Who connects in that situation is a disconnected version of you.

Lets begin your practice: Find a comfortable seated position; start tuning in to your body.

Take a deep breathe in and exhale. Tune into your physical body. What do you notice in your physical body? For example: sensations; lightness, pain, pressure, nervousness. Awareness is the first step, what is your body telling you? Give it a word. Can you put words into what are you feeling? I am noticing this physical sensation, what is your body telling you? Learn the language of your body. Now move up into your emotions. Example: When I scan my physical body I am feeling nervous; I am feeling gratitude.

Lets move into the head. What is the story playing in your head? A disbelief of, or I feel in so much alignment in my body.

Can you see how those are intrinsically connected? They affect each other. How you are feeling comes from your mind. You can resource the answers from your physical body, emotions and mental story.

THREE COLLECTIVE BREATHES: Find a comfortable position. I invite you to press your sit-bones into the chair (this is called grounding your sit-bones), roll your shoulders in your back, lengthen your spine. Bring one hand to your heart and the other to your belly. Inhale, feel the breath coming through your body, and exhale out.

MINDFULNESS OF THE BREATHE: observe each inhale and exhale, inhale and exhale through your nose. Just feel your breath. Notice something about your breath, how does it feel? shallow, deeper. Bring awareness to the breath, there is a science behind it. That can change your reality from sympathetic to parasympathetic nervous system The state of fight and flight activate our sympathetic nervous system; these practices activate the parasympathetic nervous system (rest, digest).

BELLY BREATHING: Bring your hands outside your rib-cage, inhale, expand your rib-cage, feel the movement of your rib-cage as you inhale through the nose and exhale through the nose. Pull the air all the way down; your diaphragm expands in to your sides and your rib-cage in to your lower back. A lot of your lower back issues arise because you are holding your breath. You hold tension in front of your belly.

SOMATIC BREATH WORK:
The first half is designed to be a little intense. Spiking your Nervous System; allowing you to clear out; Inhale through the mouth and exhale through the mouth. Find your own rhythm. the most beneficial breath is how far down you can pull it. In the second half you show your system how to come back in a relaxed state, you are going to inhale through your nose and exhale through the nose start to elongate your exhale. How did it feel for you?

Then inhale and exhale through your mouth three times and at the last one hold it at the top. Ask yourself, How do I feel?

The yoga of consciousness. With just few minutes of practice, helping you to slow down your movements, slow down your thoughts, slowing down the momentum. Abraham Hicks said: "When I focus on my illness I am ill. When I focus on my wellness I am well." Redirect your dialogue, whatever the dialogue is. Through yoga we discover our truth, our essence which it is love. Bringing a strong nervous system, balancing the glandular system, softening our heart, and creating an intuitive mind. We feel more confident, and our happiness will not depend on the ups and downs of life.

When the fears of the world take you out, return to the present moment, return to these tools to align with your essence which is love. Miracles only happen in the present moment.

To get started. All you need is your willingness and a chair. All your positions can be applied to any kind of chair. Sometimes we don't have a yoga mat handy. I photographed them all in a standard folding chair so that you can better see the anatomical focus and alignment of the pose.

With these chair yoga techniques you can strengthen the body, stimulate the mind, cultivate self awareness and response management skills, and regain a sense of well-being in just a few minutes a day. And lastly, it will help you to be more resilient in stressful times.

We learn to connect with our breath, body, thoughts, and emotions as we practice chair yoga. We cultivate a deeper sense of self awareness. This is the foundation of social learning competency that leads to positive life outcome.

First sit in the chair. Ground through your sit bones, lengthen your spine, roll the shoulders down and back. Bring your right hand to your heart and the left hand on the top of the right. Notice how you feel, then focus on your breath.

Moving our bodies with your breath. Being in the body so that you can express it with a word or maybe two. This is how you cultivate self awareness skills. Ask yourself how you feel, so that we can go into Response management.

Ask yourself how do you feel right now? Maybe a fearful thought? First slow your mind by slowing your breath, take deep belly breaths, counting 6 in the inhale and exhale. Inhale to catch your thoughts and calm the mind. First notice the thought, allow the thought you are having to finish. Do not resist the thought; allow it until the end. Notice the emotion, feel it to heal it. Shift your awareness and consciousness through the heart. A practical way to shift that thought to a new pathway. Its in 3 steps: 1. Be on the look out for the good, 2) save it for 20 seconds, 3) go for 3:1 ratio. 3 good things to one bad thing, its a biochemical hit to change your Neuro pathway. Recognize when you start to have negative thoughts about a situation and flip it over to finish the thought with a positive aspect.

Listen in stillness, What is your inner voice or inner wisdom wanted you to do? The Course Of Miracles said:"All decisions can be made with internal guidance".

RESPONSE MANAGEMENT:

When we are aware of how we feel, we expand our capacity to pause. Reflect, and thoughtfully respond.

You can use these practices responsively. In response to stressful moments or situations.

Proactively: As daily practice to enhance overall well-being.

You can incorporate these tools in your morning routine also. Not only in stressful times.

When you proactively integrate these tools into your morning routine, it will decrease overall reactivity.

With one minute of mindful breathing you are more connected with yourself. You can focus and learn more. Theses practices help us to be self-reliant during our stressful lives.

I invite you to join me in these practices. I will offer you different options. Creating a space so that you can be in the present moment, a consistent space to the present moment, and you will find that its OK to be in your body.

You can use this yoga for a brain break or for energizing. If you are a teacher you can use them in your classroom in transition before activities. Before a test or at the beginning of the class in order to focus. Cultivate social and emotional awareness. Practices to regulate their body and emotions later on when needed. Decreases overall reactivity. As you know the way we react to our experiences, its what is going to determine the outcome in any situation.

Let's get started! I am doing this movements with you; but I can't do it for you. And become the happiest person you know.

Breathing: move your body with the breath. Foundation of mindful movement, connecting the movement with the breath bring you to the present moment. Start to feel your breath, feel how it is to breathe right now, fascinate with your breathe. Breathe in and out through your nose

I invite you to deeply inhale. Lift your arms to the sky. And exhale, bring your hands to your heart. Do it three times.

Bring your hands to your heart and notice how you feel.

Simple breathing technique, linking the movement with the breath.

MINDFUL HEALING MOVEMENTS: Connecting the body with the mind through the breath.

As The Course of Miracles says: Healing starts when you consider another possibility.

A) WARM-UP POSTURES:

1) Shoulder Rolls with breath I invite you to take a deep Inhale as you raise your shoulders by your ears. Hold the breath for 3 seconds. Then exhale.

2) push the shoulders back and squeeze your shoulder blades, imagine you have a pencil between your shoulder blades.

3) bring your fingertips to your shoulders and make shoulder rolls forward first in one direction, and) then the opposite direction too.

4) Wrists Stretches:

Stretch your right arm straight out in front of you with the palm facing out, so the hand looks like a "high five" gesture, then take your left hand and pull the fingers of the right hand back toward the torso, holding for 60 seconds. Now turn your right hand facing down and take the left hand over the top of the right hand. Press the back of the hand down. Holding for 60 seconds.at the end turn the right palm up to face the ceiling and use the left hand to pull the fingers down for 60 seconds, Repeat everything on the left hand.

Prevent long term stress in your hands, due to a lot of typing.

Prevent carpal tunnel syndrome. You can do from 30 seconds, I minute or five minutes.

Close your eyes or soften your eyes, continue feeling your breath. I invite you to bring your hands to your heart and describe how you feel with two words. Integrate into your personal practice, Its a great way to cultivate social emotional competence and self awareness skills.

B) Bring your hand on your knee and lift the leg up, opening your hip flexors, even when you are seated, start making ankle circles, point and flex, eversion and inversion.

C) Seated Side Bends: Start by sitting at the edge of the chair, feet touching the floor with feet hip distance apart. Draw length in your spine .Bring your hands together to your heart, I invite you raise your arms up to the sky. Look up. Exhale bring right hand down , grabbing the chair as far you can go and left hand up, reach up and over, creating a side bend. Continue to breath in a way that feels good in your body. Now slowly come back. Again bring your hands to the heart, inhale, lift your arms up, maybe looking up, exhale, bring left hand down as far you can go to grab the seat and create your side bend, feel all the stretch from your sit bone to the side body, make it feel good. And slowly and mindfully come back to center.

Notice whats here now, any sensation or emotion?

Notice what you feel after the side bends and express it with two words

D) Seated Twists: bring your right hand to the left knee, left hand behind you, inhale, create length to the spine by lifting the shoulders, and create twist by looking over your left shoulder, then come back to the center. Bring your left hand to the right knee, right hand behind you, inhale, wherever it feels good for you, look over your right shoulder, inhale, lengthen the spine by lifting the shoulders, create twist by looking over your right shoulder, exhale, then come back to the center.

Creating more opening and space, you can think that you are releasing all the tension as you twist. Shift the energy.

What do you feel after the twisting?

Two words of how you feel.

I like to think that my spine is like a sponge and as I twist, it releases all the tension, so that I can see things from a new perspective.

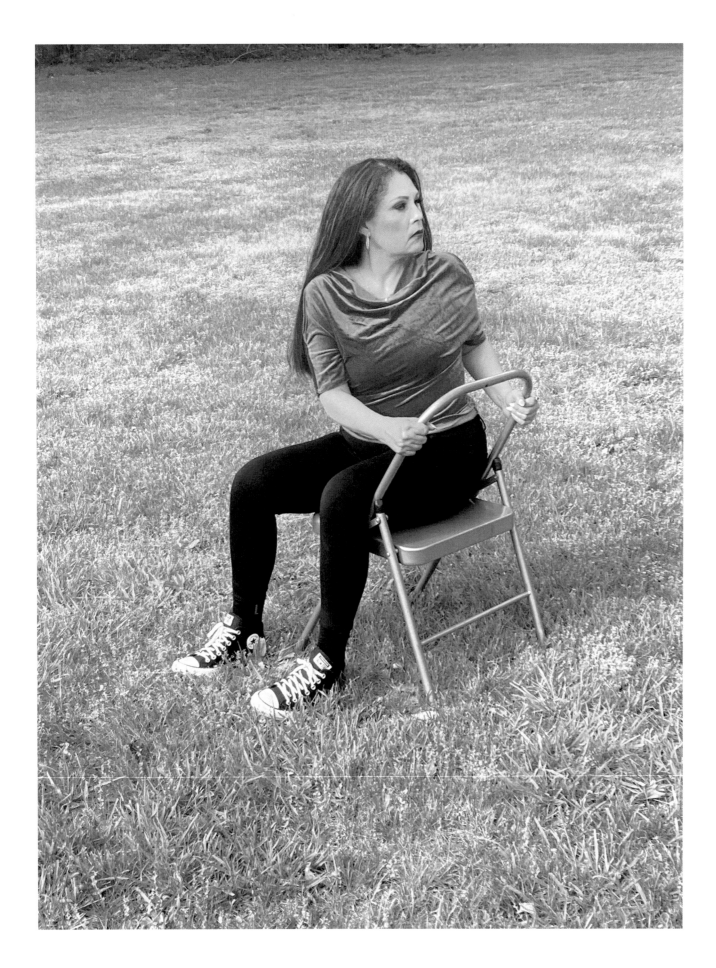

E) Half Sun Salutation: Its very simple to do it in a chair. Scoot to the front of your chair so that you feel rooted in your seat bones.

Inhale. Reach up. Exhale. Move hands to heart center and slide hands down the legs. Maybe you can go all the way down touching the floor. Inhale. Lift your hands halfway and squeeze between your squeeze between your shoulder blades. Exhale. Bend forward at the waist, arms sliding down to your legs, then straighten up and open your arms going up. Exhale, hands to your heart.

Pause and notice how you feel at this moment?

Say two words

When we ask the question how do I feel after practicing chair yoga; we support ourselves in awareness skills, but also in Response management skills. When times get challenging we observe, pause, reflect and respond.

F) Cat / Cow

Sit tall at the edge of the chair, placing your feet a hips distance apart. Place your hands on your knees.

Inhale and lengthen your spine, arching back slightly and squeezing your shoulders together. Then as you exhale, move the shoulders forward, rounding your chest and tucking your belly in.

How do you feel?

G) Figure Four in the chair:

Sit tall at the edge of the chair, placing your feet a hips distance apart.

Inhale and lift your right leg up at the level of the seat bones, Exhale and cross your right ankle at the top of your left knee, staying there for a couple of breaths, feeling comfortable in your position. Exhale and uncross the right leg and bring the foot down.

Inhale and lift your left leg up at the level of your seat bones, exhale and cross your left ankle to the top of the right knee, stay there for a couple of breaths, Exhale and uncross the left leg and bring the foot down.

How do you feel? What did come up for you? Maybe an emotion came up, hips store a lot of emotions, just observe without judgment.

CHAPTER 3:

Crisis as an Opportunity

"My Faith helps me overcome such negative
emotions and find my equilibrium"
Dalai Lama

2020 is a year that everybody will remember: COVID.
I was enjoying teaching yoga as a career yoga instructor at yoga studios, schools settings, corporations and private classes. Serving and healing my students through yoga. And suddenly COVID came. All of the yoga studios closed. So we started teach yoga classes virtually until the studios could open again.

I found myself very sad when many of the studios could not open again for yoga classes. Some of them had to declare bankruptcy. Communities that I have served for many years, I was not going to serve them anymore.

It's easy to get down by the difficulties and negativity we face, that we loose sight of the positivism altogether in ourselves and in the world. That's why it's so important to take a step back and look at things from another point of view.

As a student and teacher of the course of miracles, I practice a prayer from the book everyday: "What do you want me to do? Where do you want me to go? What do you want me to say and to whom?" Since that moment I started practicing that prayer I felt guided everyday to people and circumstances in my life.

One day I opened my Instagram account and I saw Gabrielle Bernstein guiding a meditation to relieve anxiety. For a reason that I can not explain I felt drawn toward her teachings. I continue practicing all the meditations she was offering. I felt tremendous change in me, telling everyone "All is well." People asked me "are you ok?" "We are in pandemic." "Are not you scared?" "We do not know anything about this virus, and its killing people. People are dying in the hospitals." My answer was that I can not help anyone if I am not calm. I need to regulate my nervous system so that I can contribute with my energy to the healing of the world.

Vibrations speak louder than words. Its the best contribution I can do for the world, by regulating my nervous system, and going out with good energy. Its the same as to why we put garbage in the bins instead of us throwing away garbage into the streets. We do not do it, because we care about the ecosystem. Feeling good its feeling part of the divine. Oneness requires a calm mind.

So I decided to take her master class which is for people that want to create a spiritual business, and I wanted to do that: Science and spirituality. Yoga as a science. I always love science because Science brings people together. I felt that I needed to do something, so I offered free yoga classes and I opened a book club virtually on Sundays before my yoga class. The book club is on The Course of Miracles. And when we arrive to the lesson 34 of the course of miracles it tell us, "I could see peace in this situation instead of what I think I see."

I can replace my feelings of depression, anxiety or worry with peace, shifting my perspective from the ego's self-limiting beliefs. The ego is quite literally a fearful thought.

I have never been interested much in computers, but since it was the only way I could communicate with my students, I started learning and after that teaching my students how they can navigate in their computer so that they can attend both the Chair Yoga class and the book club. And they did it.

One of my students is 72 years old. Her name is Ms. Mary. She said that she has always been active, but never as much as she is now. Ms Mary began practicing chair yoga at age 70, twice a week. She lives on her own and drives her own car. Ms. Mary drives herself wherever she needs to go.

After six months of practicing endurance of stretch and strengthening yoga postures, Ms Mary was able to perform households tasks more easily. These included carrying groceries, making her bed, and transferring laundry more quickly, She could also carry more weight.

"It just has done a world of good" Ms Mary said of her physically active lifestyle.

She wants older adults who read this book to know that, when it comes to exercise and physical activity, "there is always something that someone can do". There is no reason older people need to be just sitting in a rocking chair.

When we practice gratitude, we feel more positive emotions. We strengthen our relationships and improve our health. It can even help us better deal with adversity.

The more resilient and clear-minded we are during a crisis; the better we can show up for our loved ones and the world.

I am so grateful for my coffee in the morning, I enjoyed the taste of coffee. It makes me happy.

I am grateful for the work I do in the world and the work I am inspired to do. And also I am so appreciative for all the tough lessons and the hard times, even especially my car accident. Because if that hadn't happened to me I neither would have guided my students, nor written this book.

Focus your attention onto something you appreciate about your physical body; or about people in your life; or where you live. It could be as simple as your bed after a nice bed rest, for which Louise Hay was grateful.

ENDURANCE AND STRENGTH POSTURES

CHAIR POSE:

Stand halfway out of your seat, hips and thighs hover over the seat of your chair. Extend the arms out straight in front of the body. Hold for a couple of breaths, and then sit carefully back onto your chair.

TRIANGLE:

Lengthening the torso, opening the sides and waist, inner thighs and tones the legs and arms.

1. Start standing in front of the chair with your right foot in the middle of the chair's front legs.

2. Step your left foot back 2 to 3 feet and angle the left foot inward about 45 degrees,

3. Turn the right foot out 90 degrees. Lift your arms to the sides, parallel to the ground and hinge to the right, stretching as far as you can.

4. Place the right hand on the chair seat and extend the left arm up to the ceiling. Gaze toward the top hand and hold for 5 to 8 breaths.

Inhale to stand up and position yourself for the left side.

PEACEFUL WARRIOR

Sit tall at the edge of the chair, placing your feet a hips distance apart.

Separate your legs wide apart, lift your right leg and turn it to the right, bending at the right knee, then extend the left leg fully and straighten it. Position the left foot at a 45 degree angle.

Lift both arms to shoulder height bending your elbows with your palms up, and you can either face right or face forward, which ever is more comfortable. Let your toes point forward to the short edge of your yoga mat, knee aligned with the ankle and weight on the heel, protecting the knee.

Hold for 3 to 5 breathes.

REVERSED WARRIOR:

Starting from your Warrior II, place your left hand on your left leg, while you reach your right arm toward the ceiling, feel the stretch in your right side body. Look toward your right hand, if you feel comfortable in your neck; if not you can look down.

Hold for 3 to 5 breaths.

EXTENDED SIDE ANGLE

Start from your reverse warrior lean your torso to the right thigh, and rest your right forearm on your right thigh. Inhale, lift your left arm overhead, be mindful of not collapsing in your right shoulder, gently press your left shoulder back. Look toward your left hand if it is comfortable in your neck. Hold for 3 to 5 breaths

Turn back to center. Repeat all of the Warrior postures on your left side.

Notice how you feel after these big movements

CAMEL:

Sit tall at the edge of the chair, placing your feet a hips distance apart.

Sit at the edge of your chair. Bring your fingertips as far as possible. Expand your chest, squeeze between your shoulder blades, lift your chest toward the sky. Hold for 3 to 5 breaths and release.

EAGLE:

Sit tall at the edge of the chair, placing your feet a hips distance apart

Cross your right leg over the left, trying to lock your right toes behind your left leg. If you cannot lock your toes, just cross the right leg over the left. Spread the arms wide and move the arms to hug yourself, then place the left arm on the top of the right arm so that your elbows are stacked one on the top of the other. Move elbows away from the chest a little, with palms straight. If this is not comfortable, just place your right hand on your left shoulder and your left hand on your right shoulder, giving yourself a hug. Hold for 3 to 5 breathes. Repeat on the other side.

SPINAL TWIST:

Sit tall at the edge of the chair, placing your feet a hips distance apart.

Move both legs to the right so that the left side of your body faces the middle of the room. Place your right hand on the right side of your seat back and the left hand on the left side. Gently look toward your right shoulder. Allow your exhales to help you twist slightly deeper. Hold for five to seven breaths and then switch sides.

CHAPTER 4:

Tune Into the Loving Vibration of the Universe.

The thinking of the world is based on fear and separation

When you eliminate the concept of separation from your thoughts and your behavior, you ask "Is my heart truly open? Am I focused on service? Who do I choose to be?" You begin to feel your connection to everything and everyone. By aligning the mind with the heart, it expands our thinking.

At every moment in our lives we are choosing: fear or love consciously or unconsciously. Is my heart going to open to something much bigger that what I can see with my physical eyes. When I was a kid I used to play the game flip the coin with my dad. Heads or tails?. I went to Mexico in August 2022 to visit the basilica of the Shrine of Our Lady of Guadalupe. While at the Shrine, they suggested to me to get a coin to remember my experience, and so I did. When I looked at the coin, it showed at the front the image of Our Lady and at the back its blank. I remember the game that I used to play with my dad, but now when I flip my coin it is faith in one side and the other fear. Its up to me which side I choose to stay in any situation in my life.

Overcome fear: Every experience I have is perfect for my soul.

When we start having that illusion that we are separate from each other, then its when we experience fear(ego). Basically its how we see ourselves in relation with other people, mother earth, animals. Its not only about ourselves. I identify myself with the power of the ocean. When I am in the beach with my surfboard and if I am thinking that I am separate from the ocean I will be totally scared when a big wave comes. But since I am one with the ocean I move with flow, ease and grace.

Prayer aligns to oneness.

As a Latino woman as I love coffee and make up. A lot of color. If you have seen my pictures in social media I am always with makeup, and false eyelashes. People always tell me if I want to look natural? and I answer this is me, with a lot of color, that is natural to me, because it makes me happy who I am. In 2021 my makeup finished so I went to the mall to buy more. I left home with my spiritual gangster hat. It reminds me to be fearless, because I am a spirit living a human experience.

I arrived at the counter. Then the lady told me, "you arrived, that was so fast." I said to her, "Pardon me?"

She answered "I was praying for the right coach to guide me in this spiritual path, and you show up, your hat is my sign."

Since that day I did a connection with Anne and started guiding her creating a miracle minded success, changing her core belief, undoing her old operating system from fear into faith.

As I continue my personal growth and my spiritual development, Gabrielle Bernstein became my spiritual teacher as well as Marianne Williamson; and the spiritual sign of Gabrielle Bernstein is an owl, which it means that when we can not see clearly which way to go we get a sign, its personal, you decide, and for her has been the owl.

Every day I saw that owl everywhere I went, television, supermarkets, purses, eyeglasses, universities, etc. At the beginning I thought maybe I am pushing in my mind to see this owl, so I will relax and not listen any of her talks and just do my regular practice: yoga and meditation. But it did not stop. I could seeing her sign. At that point I sent her a DM in Instagram to her telling her what was going on with me.

I told Gabby Bernstein the following.

I keep doing my ritual in the morning. First I open my eyes in the morning. I am so grateful that I woke up that morning. Then I do my prayers and meditation, including The Course of Miracles As I continued my practice, it came to me that I am in the right path and my mission is to work in collaboration with spiritual leaders to help a new world to be born. Since that moment it became clear that I needed to write this book with the intention to invite others to do the same that are in the spiritual path. Everyone has different stories and experiences that lead us from fear to faith, even though the spiritual principles are the same. All of us can work in collaboration to create a new world. When we share an idea it becomes stronger. So many people will be attracted to my book, but others to you.

Let's so do it, lets co-create with the universe.

BALANCE POSTURES:

Balance is a state of the mind.

TREE:

Stand tall, with feet hip distance apart, extend your right leg to the side, with your toe touching the floor. Hold the chair with the left hand.

Lift your right heel to your left ankle, shin or inner thigh, avoiding any pressure on the knee, you can have your hands at your heart, or maybe your hands overhead, hold the posture for a 3 to 5 breaths, and then repeat on the left side.

How do you feel?

DANCER'S POSE:

Stand tall behind your chair, feet hip distance apart. Hold the back of the chair with your left hand. Lift the right foot back and flex at the right knee until your right leg make a 90 degree angle. Lift the right hand toward the ceiling.

Reach down with your right arm and touch or grab your right ankle. Start pushing your right foot away from your body into a bow, and hold for 3 to 5 breathes. Repeat on the other side.

How do you feel?

WARRIOR III:

Stand tall, feet hip distance apart behind your chair. Hold the chair back with your right hand, if needed grab the chair with both hands.

Lean forward as you raise your right leg until your right leg and your arms are both parallel to the floor.

If you feel confident, release the chair and bring both arms forward. Hold for 3 to 5 breathes.

Repeat on the other side.

How do you feel?

CHAIR SQUAT ON ONE LEG:

Stand tall, feet hip distance apart in front of your chair.

Place your right ankle above your left knee or calf.

Bring your arms straight out in front of you and bring your hands to heart center in prayer position while bending your knees and lowering your hips as you are sitting down onto a chair. Hold this posture for 3 to 5 breaths. Repeat on your other leg.

How do you feel?

CHAPTER 5:

"Love is letting go of fear"
Gerald Jampolsky

I have always been so passionate about vision boards, because I am a visual person. And feeling good leads us into visions. I started teaching to my students how to create a vision board. I realize they can benefit from it. Vision boards work by programming the part of the brain responsible for attention, the reticular system, by focusing your mind,

In fact my students did benefit from a vision board. We created a vision board in 2019 for the year 2020. I was so happy to hear their testimonies, that many things they posted in their vision board came through for them.

Basically my vision board represents me, and what do I want. Its aligned with my mission, so I visualized writing a book helping millions of people with it. Also to become a vehicle for social change, and being published in Hay House. The writing and publishing is now happening.

Our society is based on loveliness. A duality world.

We are the vessels for change. You rise up to become the person you are capable to be in collaboration with others. When you shine you give the permission to others to do too.

PIGEON:

Sit tall feet hip distance apart at the edge of your chair. Inhale. Place your right ankle just above your left knee. Exhale and bend forward from your hips, keeping your back flat. Hold for a few breaths, Inhale and rise up into your posture. Exhale. Repeat on the other side.

If placing your ankle over your knee is difficult, sit forward in the chair, straighten your left leg and cross your right ankle over the left ankle, and then lean forward.

How do you feel?

You have another option for your pigeon: bring the right leg into the seat of the chair, try to bring the shin parallel to the chair, and extend the left leg.

How do you feel?

HAMSTRING STRETCH:

Sit tall feet hip distance apart at the edge of your chair.

Extend your right leg so its almost straight, keep a slight bend in your knee, your right foot should remain balanced with the heel touching the floor.

Gently lean forward from your hips until you feel a stretch in the back of your right thigh. For a calf stretch, stay in this position, but do not lean forward. Keep the right heel on the floor and pull your toes up toward your shins as much as possible.

Repeat for the left side.

How do you feel?

WIDE LEG FORWARD FOLD:

Sit at the front edge of the chair. Bring your feet and knees wide apart, Place hands on the inside of each thigh, gently pressing outward. Exhale as you lean forward, hinging from the hips and keeping a flat back. Lower as much as possible, hold for 3 to 5 breathes, then inhale and straighten up.

How do you feel?

SEATED FORWARD BEND:

Sit tall at the edge of your chair feet hip distance apart.

Inhale, and lift your arms overhead. Exhale as you bend forward until you are relaxing with your chest on your lap and your arms dangling toward the floor.

Remain here for a 3 to 5 breathes. Inhale as you slowly roll up one vertebrae at the time: lower back, middle back, upper back, shoulder blades, shoulders and head. Exhale and relax your body.

How do you feel?

CHAPTER 6:

Final Relaxation and Meditation

Every yoga session finishes with a period of relaxation. But you can do this practice and stop what you're doing anytime of the day and give yourself a rest.

Final relaxation is like a deep state of rest without falling asleep.

The purpose of relaxation is to refresh the mind and absorb the benefits of your yoga practice, As you develop your practice, relaxation becomes natural, sometimes even spiritual.

I was finishing my chair yoga practice one day. So I decided to lie down on the floor, to feel the energy of mother earth. At some point I let go everything and I had a vision of my book very clear with the A of chair yoga, being the Eiffel Tower. I have never been to France. I only knew the story of love behind the Eiffel Tower. So at that moment I knew that I had to take action so I am designing the cover of my book through Canvas, to design what I saw on my vision.

Let's start:

Allow your body to become still and relax, with your back pressing gently into the back of the chair. Rest your hands on your thighs in a comfortable position and close your eyes.

Another option is to lie down in the floor and rest your legs comfortably on the seat in the chair.

MEDITATION:

Dalai Lama said: In order to heal the world we must have a plan; but he said, no plan will work; unless we meditate.

In the morning the mind is open with new impressions. Five minutes in the morning. The Holy Spirit will be in charge of your thought form during the day.

Feel the Consciousness that you are as you listen inwardly; when we meditate and pray, we align our mind with God's power. Our Nervous System takes on a mantle of peace; our anxious thoughts are replaced by peaceful ones.

Our thinking becomes brilliant.

The yoga poses I have introduced to you are mindful and slow purposeful movement.

Yoga Asanas prepares us for meditation. As we focus on the breath and preparing the body to sit erect. The Chair is perfect place to meditate.

Sit comfortable; feet flat on the floor, hip-width apart. Sit bones anchored, shoulders down and back; spine tall.

SAVASANA

Relax into the energy of love; in these moments of genuine release you can reorganize your nervous system and realign your connection with love.

HOW TO PRAY

The Course of Miracles said to pray that your perceptions can be changed.

Praying from a place of lack, we usually learned to do it in any religious settings.

Its important to Pray when things go right. Prayer - its about preparing, not asking.

You don't ask for things Ask for feelings, ask how the outcome would make you feel. Tuning into how good it feels. And take it to the next level; celebrate after your prayer practice, that your prayer is being answered. Dance with your favorite music experience what your prayer has been delivered, consider it done. Keep in that gratitude space and that is how you get your prayers answered. For example if you are trying to overcome a health situation in your life; pray "Thank you God for the healing that has already being given to my body, it feels so good to emanate health and wellness, thanks for the freedom that comes with me." Until I am overflowing, it feels so good to demonstrate to others that my body is a vehicle to miracles.

We speak that what we already asking for its already achieved, we pray as we already experience the result and the feeling that comes with that prayer being answered.

And you can apply it to any areas of your life.

Gratitude its a higher vibration

Prayer is the pathway of love by directing the mind to hear the voice of God over the voice of fear, to notice brilliant thoughts that come naturally from deeper regions of our consciousness. It expands our consciousness

A course in miracles says:"prayer is the media of miracles" and "Through prayer love is received, and through miracles love is expressed".

When you pray you offer up your ego's story, fear of the past, and future, and welcome a new perspective. And that its a miracle, a shift in perception from fear to love.

When you pray you welcome freedom from resistance. Let go and allow. You open up to an infinite field of possibilities.

There is no formula for how to pray; simply pray from your heart with sentiments such as *Dear God lift all these things into Your hands*. When one get tempted into fear, may you be guided back into loving thought; pray that love might be my experience, and love might be my power, and love might be my happiness and peace, in every single moment of my day.

Amen.
And so it is.

Surrendering does not mean I am giving up my dreams, it means I am giving over my timeline and my need to control the outcome. When we pray we give other to a faithful higher power or God. The faith offers us clear direction when we are lost.

Once we start to give others, what we think, or need, it is that moment when the universe can show up for us; that is when we experience synchronicity and support and clear direction, and it has to start with faith.

To receive Spiritual guidance, you can really start to trust every step of the plan that unfolds for you

Ask the universe for help:

"Thank you" you universe for guiding my thoughts back to love.

"Thank you universal guidance for guiding me to solutions that are of the highest good for all."

The goal is to get into a state of receptivity, a state of non resistance and allow. Abraham-Hicks call: "The art of allowing".

Thank you universe and guides of the highest truth and compassion .

I am ready to feel free, I welcome a new found faith.

Prayer from a course in miracles:

Where would you have me go?

What would you have me do?

What would you have me say and to whom?

And I suggest you to write about how it feels to give it over.

Pray Proactively: How can I be a vessel for good

Prayer of the Miracle Worker: I am willing to see this differently.

+

And take a moment to settle into the feeling of what it means to surrender to faith in the universe. The energy of faith, it is an energy of allowing.

CHAPTER 7:

Unlearning Thoughts of Fear, Replacing Them with Thoughts of Love

Quote from Rumi, "Don't move the way fear makes you move, move the way love makes you move".

Enlightenment is not a learning, but unlearning- unlearning a thought system based on limitation and fear in order to attract happiness and unlimited good. We can train our attitudinal muscles much like we exercise our physical muscles, training ourselves to think in ways that deflect fear and negativity. We can release a thought system based on fear and accept a thought system based on love instead.

Miracle-Mindedness is when we align our consciousness in such a way that positive circumstances become the norm, love flows easily, and miracles occur naturally.

Only a shift in the way we see the world will provide a shift in the way we experience it.

A Course in Miracles says we achieve so little because we have undisciplined minds, constantly lured by the thinking of the world into regions of fear and despair.

MANTRAS AND MOVEMENT: solidifying your new belief, reprogramming your subconscious based on the Course of Miracles

When we do physical exercise with weights, sets with repetitions help us to resist physical gravity and its the same concept for your mind. Its emotional gravity that pull your mind down. Do Daily repetition of thoughts that resist the emotional gravity. And in Chair Yoga first we align by stacking the bones, then we stabilize the muscles and elongate by lengthening into the pose.

To change an emotion through: 1) the thought, 2) words and 3) movement in your body When you want to change an emotion, you need to change your limiting beliefs which are the origin of every situation in your life. That is The Course of Miracles. Its a mind training for your internal peace.

A Mantra - Its a statement of truth, like planting seeds in the ground, releasing old beliefs and patterns. And replacing it with a new one.

Say it and live it, with the Chair yoga postures make the mantra as part of your body. The Mantra will let you tune in more of the present and into the flow of acceptance. Into the flow of allowing no fear. The only point where God's time intersects the linear time ; the present moment. Movement in your body creates movement in your brain to get that transformation shifting from resistance to flow. As soon as you allow to replace the fear-based beliefs with new perceptions, you receive a miracle.

Recite powerful mantras with movement, create movement in your brain. The power of movement to get that transformation, which can instantly put you into spiritual, physical and emotional alignment.

Sit in your chair, start rocking forward and backwards until you find your sit-bones, helping you to find your neutral spine, above your sit-bones keeping your spine straight. Relax your shoulders by lifting your shoulders up to your ears and then bring them back.

Keep your hips aligned with your knees, if your legs are short, bring any support underneath your feet to keep the hips in alignment with the knees. feet parallel, knees aligned with your ankles. Heels aligned with second and third toe. Press down the four corners of your feet; lift the inner arches.

Bring the arms parallel with palms facing up. Inhale lift both arms up, and say: I am. Exhale and bring palms together and close to your heart and say love. Repeat as much as you can until you feel the spirit of love flow through you.

Side to Side with Neck: As you inhale, move your head to the right and say: I am one with God, exhale bring head to the left and repeat: I am one with God. Be gentle. Every time you move your head; see if you can go further. May be a different place each time.

Sun Salutation with folds:

Sit at the edge of your chair and start the inhalation as you lift your arms overhead; I breathe God's love as you exhale, hinge at your hips and fold over your legs until your torso drops over your lap or your hands come into the floor; I dwell in peace.

As you start to inhale, use your abdominal to lift your torso back up and reach the arms overhead. Exhale and bring your arms to your sides. There is nothing to fear.

Sun Salutation with Side Bends

Sit at the edge of the chair with your feet hip-width apart and firmly on the earth ,back straight.

Inhale and lift your arms overhead; maybe press your palms at the top.

Exhale and side bend to your left, dropping your left arm alongside as you stretch your right arm overhead and say it to yourself: I am an idea in the mind of God. Inhale, and back up to press palms overhead. Exhale and side bend to your right; dropping your right arm alongside as you stretch your left arm overhead and repeat: I am an idea in the mind of God.

Sun Salutation with Twists:

Sit tall with your feet hip-width apart and firmly on mother earth, your back straight. Inhale reaching the arms up overhead maybe pressing palms

As you exhale, drop your arms down and around as you twist to your left. Bring the left hand behind you and the right hand on the left knee. And repeat: I am blessed as a child of God.

Inhale back to center with arms up. Exhale and twist to the right bringing the left hand onto the right knee and the right hand behind you and repeat: I am blessed as a child of God.

Warrior II:

Sit toward the edge of the chair and toward the middle of the seat, so you can pivot to the left to sit on your right side and Extend your left leg off the chair and back behind you. Open your hips to the right so that you can bend your right knee until the thigh is resting on the seat; keep the knee aligned with the ankle. Press the left foot on the earth in an angle of 45 degrees; press firmly the outside of the foot; to lift the inner arch of the left foot.

Stretch both arms out to the sides and look over your right fingers. As you inhale repeat: I am willing to see this differently.

Come back to center and pivot to the right to seat on your left side and extend your right leg off the chair and back behind you. And repeat: I am willing to see this differently.

Reverse Warrior II:

You are coming into a seated warrior II position. Bring the left hand down to rest on the left leg. Inhale and bring the right arm up towards the ceiling, and reach the fingers away from each other. Look straight ahead or up the sky. Keep the right knee bent, Breath and repeat: I am a miracle worker.

Now keep it dynamic: from warrior II you will repeat: I am willing to see this differently and from reverse warrior II repeat: I am a miracle worker.

Extended Side Angle:

You are in a seated Warrior II position. Bring your right forearm on your right knee with the palm facing upward; move the torso a little bit to your right, extend the left arm up alongside the left ear, overhead in the direction of the right knee. Keep the neck long and say to yourself: I am entitled to miracles.

Repeat on the left side.

Now make it dynamic: starting from Extended side angle and repeat: I am entitled to miracles. And coming back to reverse warrior saying: I am a Miracle worker.

Extended Triangle:

Stand in front of the chair with your right foot in the middle; step your left foot back as wide as you can and straighten both legs with the left foot inward 45 degrees. Align the front knee with the second toe, hinge from the crease of the front hip; elongate the spine, Lengthen both sides of the waist.

Place the right hand on the seat of the chair and extend the left arm up to the sky creating a straight line. From the bottom hand to the top hand, Gaze toward the top hand. As you inhale repeat: I am as God created me.

Tree

Focus in one point in front of you. Hold on to the chair with the right hand if you need help with balance. Ground firmly into the four corners of the right foot; imagine the foot is the roots of your tree. Draw the abdominal in and straighten the right leg, square the hips to the front of your room. And lift all four sides of the torso evenly.

Take your left foot and press it to the right heel, calf or upper inner right thigh and turn the knee out to the right side. As you Inhale say: support is all around me; relax the shoulders and imagine that angels are pulling your head toward the blue sky. As you inhale say: Support is all around me. Repeat on the left side.

Warrior I:

Stand next to the chair, and get the support you need by placing your right hand on the chair.

Feet are wide enough apart so that the front thigh is parallel to the floor; the knee aligned with the ankle; align the feet heel to heel with the front foot facing forward and the back foot angled forward at about 75 degrees.

Try to keep your hips forward facing and lift your arms up above your ears with the palms facing each other. Or the right hand on the chair and just lift the left arm and press shoulder blades into the chest, and spread the collarbones. If you wish bring palms together and look up to the sky and say: In my defenselessness my safety lies.

Intense Side Stretch Pose:

stand in front of your chair with right foot forward and your left foot about half a leg's length behind you align the feet heel to heel. Press the outer edge of the left foot down and hinge forward at your waist placing your hands on the seat, or at the top of the chair. Square the hips; the front hip pins back and in while the back hip rotates forward with a back flat; maybe you lay your chest over your front thigh for an even deeper stretch.

Keep your back long and both legs straight. Create a line of energy from the base of the spine out through the crown of your head with the mantra:

I take action from spiritual alignment, that love might guide my path.

Now take dynamic movements: From Warrior I with the front knee bend , then straight it forward and Repeat with each movement: my mind reflect God's love.

Warrior III:

Start seated toward the middle of the seat crossing over; extend the left leg behind you with the toes pressing into the floor. Lean forward until you can lift your back leg up off the floor. Stretch your arms straight back or out to the sides. And repeat: I am not a body. I am free.

Downward -Facing Dog:

Stand facing the seat of the chair and place your hands shoulder-width apart. Wrists parallel to the front edge of the chair; Walk your feet back until feet hip distance apart, press the thighs back as you lengthen through the top of the sternum. Press down through the four corners of your feet; and lift the inner and outer arches; press the palms down, and lift the forearms up away from the floor. if your hamstrings are tight; you can bend the knees to lengthen the spine. And say: I choose to awaken from the delusions of the world.

Pigeon:

Stand facing the front of the chair. Place your outer right calf on the seat of the chair with the knee toward the outside of the right hip and the foot as parallel to the chair. Keep the foot flex to protect the knee. Gently bring your left leg back until you get settled onto the outer upper hip and repeat: God goes with me wherever I Go.

If you want to practice your balance: place your outer calf on the upper edge of the chairback; stand tall and keep your abdominals engage.

Savasana:

Lie down on your back; and bring your hips toward the base of the chair. Place your legs up on the chair with your knees bent parallel to the floor. And repeat to yourself:

I surrender my mind to God

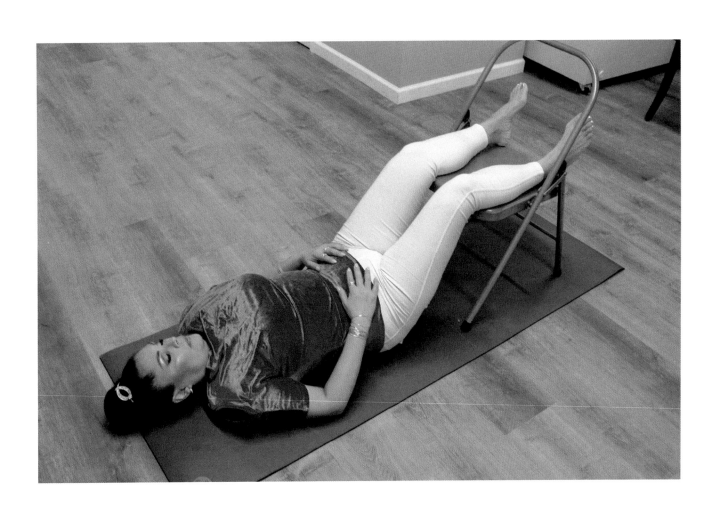

I love to give people support in my Instagram page (Alba.Nagurney)
and Facebook page (@Alba-Nagurney)

Printed in the United States
by Baker & Taylor Publisher Services